Lee Hoiby

PIANO ALBUM

Cover drawing by Robert Beers

G. SCHIRMER, Inc.

Distributed by
Hal Leonard Publishing Corporation
7777 West Bluemound Road P.O. Box 13819 Milwaukee, WI 53213

T0051121

to Stanley Babin

Narrative

Lee Hoiby, Op. 41

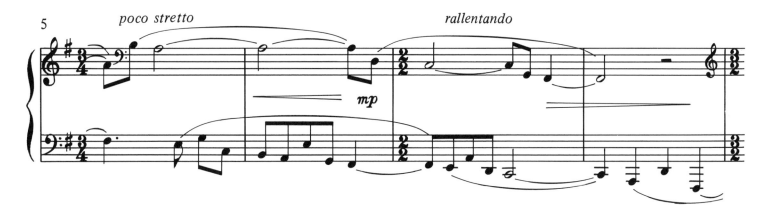

for Robert Beers

Schubert Variations

Lee Hoiby, Op. 35

*No. 3 of 17 German Dances; Deutsch - Verz. 366

Variation 1
Grazioso

22

Variation 9
Con moto, rubato ($\natural$ = c. 48)

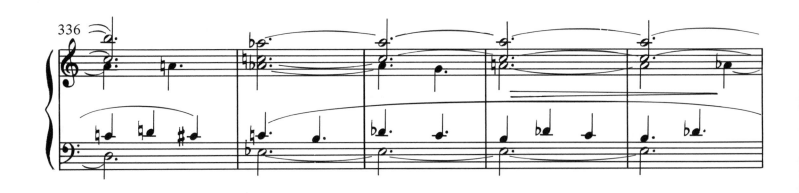

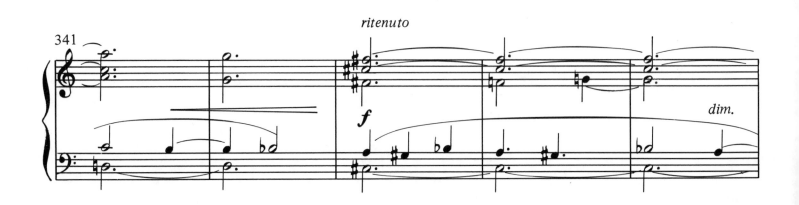

Variation 10
Allegro inquieto

Nocturne

Lee Hoiby, Op. 6

1950 Rev, 1980

Toccata

Lee Hoiby, Op. 1
(1926 -   )

Allegro molto

Piano

staccato

53

* optional cut

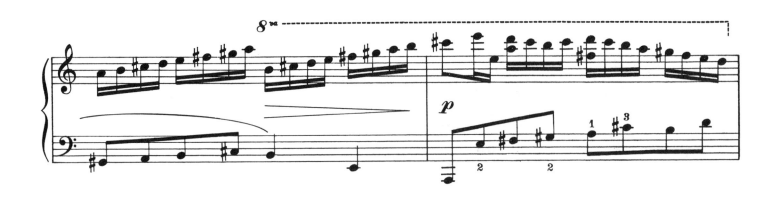

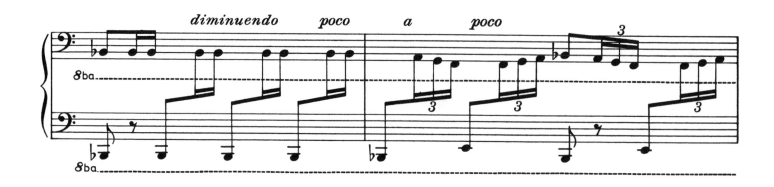

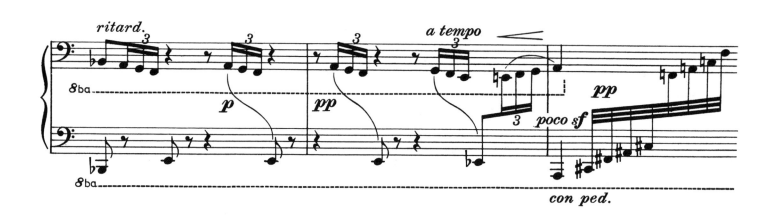

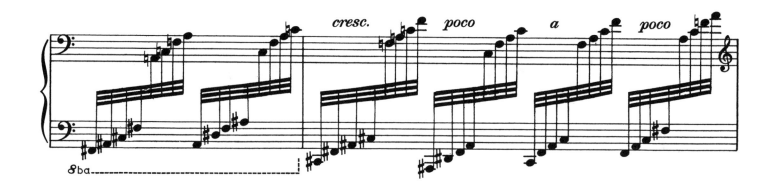

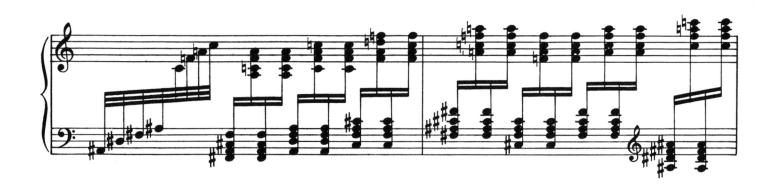

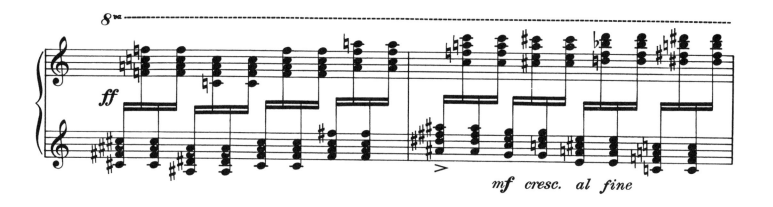

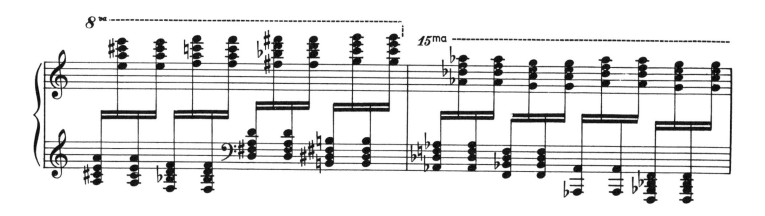

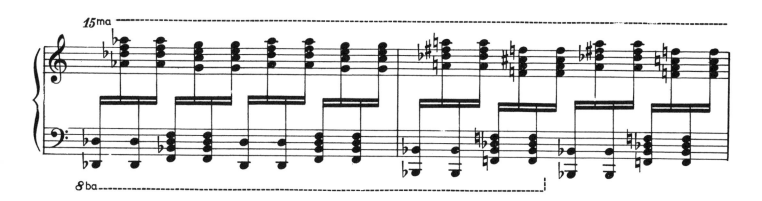

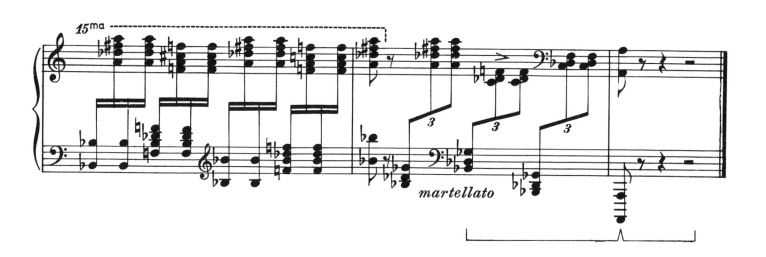